YESTERDAYS

In the same series

Yesterdays: The Way We Were 1919–1939
by Eric Midwinter

YESTERDAYS

Our Finest Hours

1939–1953

Eric Midwinter

SOUVENIR PRESS

941.083

First published 2001 by
Souvenir Press Ltd
43 Great Russell Street, London WC1B 3PD

Reprinted 2002

ISBN 0 285 63585 9

Typeset in Great Britain by Photoprint, Torquay

Printed in Singapore

CONTENTS

Introduction: *War Then Peace*   7

War and Peace: The Passing Scene   13

Change of Address   25

Making Do   35

Home Comforts   43

Women and Children   53

Queuing: 'A Characteristic Social Institution'   61

On Pleasure Bent   65

Liberty Hall   77

The Real End of the War   85

INTRODUCTION
War Then Peace

3 September 1939 – On that fateful, cloudy, Sunday morning everyone was waiting for Neville Chamberlain's announcement of the outbreak of war, fearing its inevitability, yet hoping that, somehow, war might have been avoided. The rainy morning of *2 June 1953* heralded another occasion of national expectation. This time spirits were high; we were celebrating the coronation of Queen Elizabeth II. The fourteen momentous years between span the Second World War and its difficult aftermath, a chapter of bonding in the saga of the British people for it was a time when everyone shared a common resolve, a keenness to win the war, and, afterwards, an eagerness to build a decent peace.

For Britain, at least, the suffering, marked though it was, was not so extensive in the 1939–45 hostilities as it had been in the blood baths of the 1914–18 war. Then, over 900,000 British and British Empire servicemen were killed, while in this longer second war 373,000 died. To that number, however, we must add a further 93,000 civilian deaths, compared to relatively few in the earlier war. Indeed, the aerial terror bravely borne by civilians was often as terrible as the risks withstood by servicemen. It was Britain's first real taste of total war.

The totality of war meant that all citizens were at the constant behest of the government. Their day-by-day lives were determined by a stream of governmental edicts, directing them, restricting their foodstuffs, limiting their movement, blacking out their homes, and imposing Allied as well as British personnel on their neighbourhoods. It was always logical and purposeful, if, at times, a trifle heavy-handed. By 1943, for instance, there was one rationing officer for every 400 households. No one was left free of bureaucracy's coils. If it were not rationing, conscription and direction of labour, there was a veritable bombardment of advice and instruction from the government and its officials. The entire nation, even unto its remotest crannies that had resisted change for centuries, submitted itself to vast alteration.

This phase of social history lasted longer than the war itself. This was because many of the determining circumstances remained the same. Thus, the period from the beginning of the Second World War to the mid 1950s was one of enormous social similarity, consequent on the leverage of war and its aftermath.

Rationing remained a feature of British life until the 1950s and was even more severe after 1945, when wheat and fuel shortages caused grave problems. These arose, first of all, because of the need to bring succour to liberated but starving Europe. The Americans, already anxious about the machinations of Stalin and the need to keep Western Europe on their side, diverted supplies to the continent. Then the Japanese war suddenly ended – the atom bomb, according to some experts, curtailing the war by fifteen months. The United States at once stopped their lend-lease aid to the United Kingdom, bringing further pressure on already short supplies.

Throughout this time there was continued disruption and movement of people. The wholesale uprooting of communities through evacuation, war work and military service was followed by the demobilisation of the armed forces and the return home of many workers who had been directed elsewhere on essential war work. Many households, among them those hit by wartime bombing, had to be relocated. The immediate postwar era saw families making their homes in so-called 'prefabs', while a busy start was made to create new towns and new council housing estates. Nor were clothing, furniture and other household goods abundant, for it took time to adapt the manufacturing war-machine to peace-time purposes. Times remained hard: 'Austerity' and 'We Work or Want' are post-1945 maxims.

Also current then was a firm belief in the virtues of high levels of public service and rational planning. What was known as 'War Socialism' – the national control of, for instance, hospitals, railways and fire services during the Second World War – eased the subsequent post-war nationalisation of staple industries, like coal mines, railways, gas, electricity and water. This was particularly the case with the Welfare State, in some respects a co-ordination of the social agencies created during the war. There was a whole-hearted welcome for the National Health Service. At least, the people at large welcomed it; the medical profession, marshalled by 'the Radio Doctor', Charles Hill, in his day-job guise as Secretary of the BMA, was not so happy about it. All in all, however, the notion of public and collective provision remained intact.

There was a certain continuity from wartime to peacetime politics. While Winston Churchill had magnificently rallied the people with his superb rhetoric and concentrated his inventive talents on the martial scene, with Conservatives like Anthony Eden and Lord Beaverbrook as his henchmen, it was his Labour colleagues in the wartime Coalition ministry who took main charge of the home front. In particular, there was the laconic Clement Attlee, who, as deputy prime minister managed the entire range of domestic action, Ernie Bevin, organising the wartime labour force with undeniable authority while laying the foundations for improved working conditions thereafter, and Herbert Morrison, responsible for home affairs and security, and developing his already percipient flair for both central and local governmental activity. This trio, along with the irrepressible Aneurin Bevan, were to be the driving force of 'the silent revolution' of the 1945–51 Labour administration. Everyone already knew their faces – there was a reassuring feeling of familiarity about the new government.

A strange quiescence characterised the social ambience during both the war and the early post-war years. Family and street codes prevailed, and streets were free of the 'incivilities' of the present time: graffiti, vandalism, incessant noise. Crime figures for the first five post-war years dropped by 5% on earlier years. Sadly, they began to spring upwards in the 1950s. War had produced its own crop of civil offences, such as black-out infringements, of which there were a million, while there were also the black market and some looting from damaged or abandoned properties. Although it would be facile to describe the times as those of chirpy innocence, crimes of violence were rare. There were less than 5,000 a year during the 1940s and early 1950s; by 1968 the figure had risen to 21,000 – and now it is over 100,000 a year.

This more patient, well-humoured spirit made the queue the dominant social symbol of the age. Housewives queued for scarce foodstuffs and other products, just as, in 1940, soldiers queued for boats to take them off the Dunkirk beaches. Weary leisure-seekers queued in trails round cinemas and football grounds; everyone queued for buses. People joined queues almost automatically. Tales were told of women queuing, as they thought, for rare oranges, only to find, when reaching the front of the line, that they were expected to give a pint of blood. It seems now a tiresome process – and, of course, it was – but acceptance of it betokened a people much readier to co-operate and share than was to be the case after 1953.

Leisure offers yet another illustration of this social continuum. Leisure expenditure zoomed upwards during and after the war: money spent on entertainments rose by roughly 120% between 1938 and 1944 and there were similar returns for the immediate post-war years. Apart from an understandable wartime 'eat, drink and be merry' mentality, less money was spent on food because of rationing, and consumption fell by an eighth during the war. This was also true of clothing and household items, where falls were even more marked. This increased outlay on recreation continued after the war, with the help of many workers' improved wages and the spending of allied troops, especially affluent GIs.

On what pleasures did they spend all this money? People found lots to occupy them in their limited free time during and after the war: in sport, in theatres and cinemas, in pubs, in dance halls. Spectator sports had a boom; 'the golden age of radio' continued; the crooned ballads and ballroom dance tunes remained the staples of popular music. Radio, in particular, consolidated its firm hold on the national psyche,

with its 'received pronunciation' now heard in virtually every home, and with its instantly recognisable leading personalities. Cinema ticket sales maintained the same high levels from the late 1930s through to the early 1950s.

Perhaps the most overt sign that 1945 did not bring an end to the post-1939 era was the continued presence of troops. Both during the war and afterwards, British armed forces and those of our allies were everywhere, reaching the further points of the islands, where their arrival was often the first sign of upheaval since time immemorial. Because conscription persisted in peacetime and American armed forces continued to be billeted on these islands in the wake of the Cold War, not much altered after 1945. Britain was a land dotted with 'home' and 'away' military uniforms. In any event, 'peace' was never an absolute; British troops were soon enmeshed in hostile action in parts of the disintegrating British Empire such as Malaya, while the 1950–53 Korean War, with British losses, falls squarely within our timespan.

As for social relationships, the loosening of moral shackles, so often the accompaniment of war, also continued in peacetime. Divorces boomed during the war, from under 10,000 in 1939 to 25,000 in 1945, and continued to climb in number over the next years. War and its aftermath make for chaotic circumstances. There were hasty courtships, brief honeymoons, maybe on the husband's embarkation leave. Unlike before the war when couples had long engagements and were often near-neighbours, now they were barely acquainted, and with husbands away at the war, many wives were lonely. Divorce had always been an expensive process, but now that higher wages were available, it became more of a possibility; there was, too, a charitable decision to permit cheaper divorces to forces personnel.

Several of these social characteristics were, of course, precursors of larger changes to come after 1953, changes which, in concert, would create a totally different Britain. The less inhibited approach to personal relationships anticipated the forthcoming 'sexual revolution'; the 'spiv' looked ahead to escalating crime rates; the elegant 'New Look', after square shoulder-pads and short skirts, presaged a return to femininity, and to woman's conventional role as housewife and mother - until the first wave of feminism came with the widespread use of the Pill in the 1960s. With India's struggle for independence, realised in 1947, the withdrawal from Empire had begun, to reach its critical point in the débâcle of Suez in 1956. Between 1939 and the early 1950s, there were huge wage rises, hinting at the hedonism of the Macmillan period at the end of the 1950s, when we had 'never had it so good'. The huge rise in private car ownership would be a major example of this. American influences, starting with Glenn Miller and carried forward by the likes of England's own Ted Heath, were shifting popular music's centre of gravity from the serenity of the dance floor towards the Rock'n'roll years. Soon Bill Haley and the Comets arrived with their vivid rendition of *Rock around the clock*.

Most crucial of all was the coming dominion of television. By the mid 1950s it was already the principal medium of popular entertainment. Variety theatre was dying and radio and cinema, apparently so inviolate, came under sudden threat. TV was to become the nation's favourite cultural medium. The coronation in 1953 not only bravely ushered in a new era, it engendered the stampede for television sets. Thousands of older people have described how they or their parents bought or rented their first-ever television set to peer at the muzzy images of that solemn event, often in extended family/neighbour groups. It has been estimated that over 20.5 million people, close on half the population, watched on approximately 5 million sets. They were gazing into a future very different in tempo and style from the one then ending.

Those years between 1939 and 1953 were years of hope. In the anticipation, even at moments of extreme peril, of eventual victory, and then in the anticipation of a just and fair peace, hope had collectively reigned. This has been called 'a sense of crusading idealism' that brought 'virtually to all a feeling of involvement in national affairs'. It was a quality that was to be increasingly muffled in the following era, with its more intense concentration on individualism and consumerism. In 1951 the Festival of Britain put its seal on this phase of the nation's story: 'the Festival was a testimony to a people still vital and vigorous in its culture, still at peace with itself and secure in its heritage'. Our finest hours stretched, then, from the Battle of Britain to the Festival of Britain.

WAR AND PEACE: THE PASSING SCENE

The Second World War brought 'total war' with a vengeance. Not since 1745, when Bonnie Prince Charlie's Jacobite Rebellion had been brutally thwarted, had Britain experienced the suffering of war at such close hand. It is true there had been bombing by Zeppelin airships in the 1914–18 war, but this had been a limited nuisance. A thousand civilians had lost their lives: bad enough, of course, but a tiny number compared with the close on 100,000 air-raid deaths of the 1939–45 war. The abiding 'sound' memory of those times is the eerie, mournful wail of the siren, still guaranteed to chill the blood of a generation – just as the universal 'smell' memory of the age is the rubbery odour of the claustrophobic gas mask, 38 million of which were hurriedly distributed with the command they should be carried at all times.

The whole landscape was changed. The air-raid shelter became as commonplace as the kitchen. The simple corrugated-iron Anderson shelter was a masterstroke: 2.25 million of these family bolt holes were made available to the quarter of households with gardens, along with 500,000 indoor Morrison shelters, in the form of a strengthened table for those with no gardens. Communal trenches and shelters were built, while, famously, 79 London tube stations, despite initial government displeasure, were used by 177,000 people at peak times. Even so a 'shelter census' at the time showed that 60% of Londoners preferred taking a chance inside their own home rather than using any kind of shelter. Something like 5 million people were engaged in civil defence, much of it full-time, with most other adults called on to undertake fire-watching duties. This uniformed vigilance underlined the total commitment to the war effort.

Barrage balloons sailed, calm and corpulent, above cities and ports, and there were sandbags and 'static water' containers everywhere. Even the humble pillar-box had its coating of ochre gas-detection paint. Along the coastline and on many open spaces there were concrete bastions and timber baulks to foil sea-borne or aerial invasion. Signposts and other geographical indicators were removed to foil spies, at least until the safer days of 1943. At nights the streets were darkened, although masked torches, headlights, and 'glimmer lighting' at busy intersections were soon permitted to reduce the crop of road accidents. In any event, most of the traffic on those dusky roads was for military or civil defence use, with many private vehicles requisitioned or, in the wartime coinage, 'commandeered'. Petrol rationing reduced the amount of civilian driving and that continued after the war, especially in the gruelling winter of 1946/7 when even the basic petrol ration was abolished, except for motorists living more than two miles from public transport.

That changed landscape survived the actual end of the war. The continuing demands of national service and the weighty presence of American service personnel ensured that Britain remained something of an armed and uniformed camp.

The day war became inevitable A despondent news vendor on the evening of Friday, 1 September 1939

Photo: Popperphoto

The proclamation of the state of war This was made on Monday, 3 September 1939 from the steps of the Royal Exchange, London. Note the City policemen are wearing tin hats and carrying gas masks

Photo: Popperphoto

Signs are painted out on railway stations From 30 May 1940 it became an offence to display a sign or direction, such was the fear of invaders, spies, and 'fifth columnists' as likely Nazi supporters were called. Railway stations within 20 miles of vulnerable coasts were unnamed; elsewhere three-inch lettering was the norm. These bans lasted until the autumn of 1942 in towns and the summer of 1943 in the countryside

Photo: Popperphoto

No, this is not really an ice-cream kiosk A camouflaged pill box on the south coast, part of the growing circles of concrete bastions built to defend 5,000 miles of coastline – the week beginning 7 September 1940 was probably the most anxious time in terms of possible invasion

Photo: Robert Hunt

The alien's town Why does a small northern town find itself completely surrounded by barbed wire entanglements and armed guards? There are grave worries in the first year of the war about enemy aliens, Nazi and other anti-British sympathisers, and this leads to the blanket internment of over 70,000 foreigners, many of them on the run from Nazi Germany. Fortunately, this prison camp is only temporary

Photo: Black Star/Robert Hunt

Blitz tube shelter London Underground stations are used as shelters from the Blitz, with this one having the line filled in. Several such used or unfinished stretches become shelters, including one incomplete extension from Liverpool Street that holds 10,000 people

Photo: Imperial War Museum/Robert Hunt

Aldwych, the morning after
Aldwych, London, during the 1940/1 Blitz. This illustrates a combination of valiant efforts to deal with the overnight damage, and the insistence of others to get to what is almost certainly vital war work

Photo: Public Record Office/Robert Hunt

Coventry mass burial On 14 November 1940 Coventry is subjected to a 10-hour aerial attack, begun with an incendiary raid to light the target, during which 554 people are killed, over a quarter of the city's housing is wrecked and the transport and telephone systems more or less put out of action. Our worst expectations are realised with the sight of a mass burial service in a British provincial city

Photo: Black Star/Robert Hunt

Bedford military vans line the streets The ceaseless endeavour of many thousands of factory workers doggedly provide the sinews of war. Such is the productiviity of the Vauxhall motor works in Luton that both sides of the main roads adjacent to the plant have to be used for the never-ending flow of new vehicles

Photo: Robert Hunt

The US invasion of Britain In September 1942, the idyllic English countryside is invaded by the vehicles, tramping feet and strange accents of American soldiers training in readiness for the Second Front

Photo: Popperphoto

CHANGE OF ADDRESS

The declaration of war in 1939 stirred the movement of population like pushing a stick into an ant hill. First, there was the movement of troops. 1.4 million were called up in 1940 alone. Men, who all their life, had travelled little further than their nearest seaside resort found themselves undergoing pilot instruction in Canada or fighting the Japanese in Singapore. Some 560,000 servicemen returned to British shores from Dunkirk in 1940, of whom 200,000 were non-British, the beginnings of a huge incursion of foreign personnel into Great Britain, including well over a million from the American forces from 1942 onwards.

What was more surprising was the amount of civilian mobility. Evacuation involved 3.5 million people – 'the biggest shift in population England had ever seen'. This comprised 2 million who evacuated themselves privately and 1.5 million official evacuees, including 800,000 children, at a weekly billeting allowance of 8s 6d (42p) a week. During the quiet 'phoney war' phase, many returned home, only to be re-evacuated when the bombing began in earnest, whilst another 300,000 left the coastal areas most vulnerable to the hazard of German invasion. Towards the end of the war, the vicious force of VI and V2 bombs led to a third evacuation of families from London. Moreover, the authorities had made one egregious double error: they had exaggerated the likelihood of massacre to a darkly ludicrous extent and had ordered makeshift coffins by the thousand, but they had somehow forgotten that property would be damaged and little preparation had been made for that. Thus, for example, one Londoner in six was made homeless in the Blitz and only one house in ten in inner London escaped damage. Nationally, 220,000 houses were completely destroyed and many more rendered temporarily inhabitable.

Then there was direction of labour, with millions of men and women coerced into war work, often far away from home. Unbelievably, during the six war years there were 60 million changes of address among the civilian population. Nor was this ebb and flow stilled in 1945. Demobilisation brought another sudden rush of change, with couples who had met in war conditions settling in different areas or, like the GI brides, sailing overseas. Apart from over 2 million families in war-damaged homes just roughly patched up, there were 300,000 families living in condemned houses, for, of course, there had been no domestic building replacement during the war. New housing, therefore, led to continued population mobility. A hundred and sixty thousand Portal houses, better known as prefabs, were speedily erected, while, just after the war, there were as many as 50,000 squatters, very newsworthy in their day, living on about 1000 unused military installations. The government managed to have 560,000 new houses constructed by 1949, while another million houses had been repaired. By the early 1950s there were over 1 million newly built homes, 970,000 of them council houses and another 180,000 private properties.

Most dramatic of all were the new towns that were proudly, if sometimes controversially, built. In 1946 fourteen sites for new towns were announced. Over the years, these additional new towns were to proffer a brand-new lifestyle to the thousands who optimistically left urban blight behind them.

Blitz aftermath The heavier bombs, dropping up to 2,500 kilograms, or land mines dangling from parachutes generate powerful blast effects, as depicted here with a bus tossed against the side of a partly demolished building. Many people leave the large cities to avoid catastrophes like this

Photo: Camera Press/Robert Hunt

Registering for war work This row of 20-year-old girls are about to register for work in the forces, on the land, in civil defence or in factories. Seven and a half million women are mobilised, the majority leaving home, often exchanging lowly jobs in domestic service, sweat shops or the retail trade for much more challenging tasks

Photo: Black Star/Robert Hunt

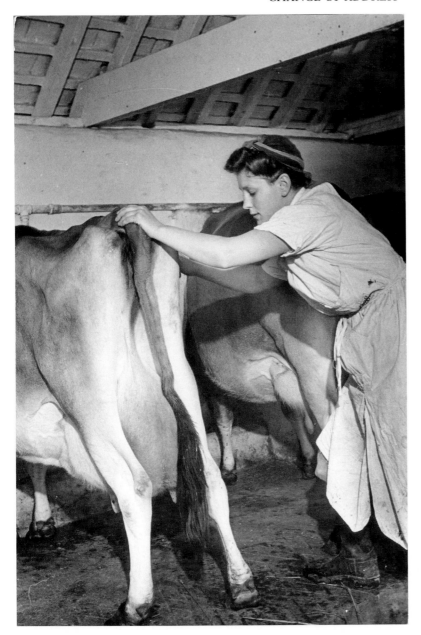

From shoe shop to cowshed
While German women –
mothers of the nation – are very
ineffectively mobilised, if at all,
British women are in the thick of
the struggle, none more so than
the 80,000 Land Army girls.
Here is a typical example of a
young woman acting the role of
milkmaid just a few weeks after
being an assistant in a Dolcis
shoe shop – and earning down
on the farm just £1.8s. (£1.40p.)
for a 50-hour minimum week

Photo: Black Star/Robert Hunt

Fear of enemy infiltration Of course, the British have to be careful about refugees arriving from the Continent, like this woman, but this uniformed confrontation does have an unbending, totalitarian air . . . despite the use of cloakroom tickets for vouchers

Photo: Black Star/Robert Hunt

Evacuees arriving in the countryside Here a London school arrives in its host township in the countryside, gas-masked and suitably labelled, ready for processing. The tales of evacuees range wildly from instances where life-long family friendships are affectionately bonded to grim examples of exploitation and abuse

Photo: Robert Hunt

Demob July 1945 and a group of RAF personnel are demobilised from Kirkham in Lancashire, some of them having donned their 'demob' suits, while others carry their £12 worth of 'civvies' in parcels. Note these are older men, for the scheme, started a week after VE Day on 18 June, is carefully geared to age, length of service, the urgent need of reconstruction work and so on

Photo: Popperphoto

Prefab: Croydon There are 160,000 of these prefabs, serviceable dwellings that will endure much longer than is originally planned, all with the then much rarer attraction of a garden. A young couple, still in uniform, stroll down the path of this Croydon prefab

Photo: Popperphoto

Squatters: Peterborough The housing shortage leads to desperate measures as ex-servicemen and their families commandeer defence properties for themselves, and the authorities respond but mildly. These 'squatters', a new word that will later take on slightly different connotations, have taken up residence in some unoccupied army huts in 1946

Photo: Popperphoto

New town: Crawley A familiar post-war scene of bustling building activity. This is the new town of Crawley in 1953, where houses are erected at the rate of 1,000 a year

Photo: Popperphoto

MAKING DO

Take a bow, S.P. Vivian, then the Registrar General, an unlikely figure in the history of British *cuisine*. In 1939 his plan for national registration, rejected at the time of the First World War, was introduced. It was another device that outlasted the war and, for the older generation, their identity numbers are still their NHS medical numbers. S.P. Vivian hoped his new system would be used directly for food rationing, about which the public were more enthusiastic than the authorities, just as they preferred orderly call-up to the chaotic volunteering of the previous war. But the authorities did not act in the straightforward manner advocated by S.P. Vivian, opting instead for another system, the buff-coloured ration book, although they had to utilise national registration for its distribution. By deploying the outmoded 1914-18 mechanism of linking customer to retailer, they saddled the British with a cumbersome method, with thousands of food office clerks tracking down changes of retailer as people made those millions of changes of address. It was a bureaucratic nightmare. When the more commercially minded Lord Woolton became minister for food, he introduced the notion of personal coupons or 'points' for jam, tinned goods and sweets. You could buy these wherever you wanted and it has to be said that the wholesale distribution of food was rarely a problem. Rationing and the hefty subsidies on food were based on sound nutritional principles and the nation's health improved, dramatically in the case of dental hygiene. In some ways, it grew worse *after* the war. The sudden end of American lend-lease, the wish to shift supplies to a badly oppressed Europe and a run of desperate weather, worldwide as well as in Britain, led to short-

ages. For example, the 1948 weekly meat ration of 13 ounces was half the wartime average, while, amid public incredulity, bread, flour and cakes were rationed for two years from July 1946. It was 1950 before 'points' rationing disappeared; fats remained rationed for still longer, and sweets and chocolate were rationed until the mid-1950s.

One marked effect of wartime rigour was the increase in communal feeding, in military messes, in factories – industrial canteens surged from 1,500 in 1939 to 18,500 in 1944 – and in schools, where the uptake of meals rose twelvefold during the war, with, by 1945, one in three children 'on school dinners'. The Blitz led to more communal eating, with London boasting 400 meals centres and mobile canteens. The British Restaurants – another of Winston Churchill's bright labels – run by local authorities and offering a hot two-course meal for 10d (4p), numbered 2,000 by 1943 and served 600,000 meals a day. All in all, 170 million communal meals were consumed each year.

One's very house and garden became a war weapon. Salvage drives denuded the home of railings, waste paper, books and kitchen utensils, while 'Digging for Victory' was all the rage. Some 600,000 new allotments almost doubled the pre-1939 total; 10 million leaflets were issue on the subject in 1942 alone; and by 1945, 1.25 million poultry-keepers, caring for 12 million birds, provided a quarter of the fresh egg supply. Of course, rationing and shortages gave rise to some excursions into the black market, with buying from 'under the counter' very much a wartime euphemism. In the wings stood the 'spiv', the dissolute trader, ready to latch on to people's greed and gullibility.

Every town has a food office Such offices are the focus of a fair but complex paperchase of ration books, coupons and points, supplementary ration cards for, among others, miners, farm workers or nursing mothers, and temporary ration cards to meet the needs of the many people on the move during the war

Photo: Robert Hunt

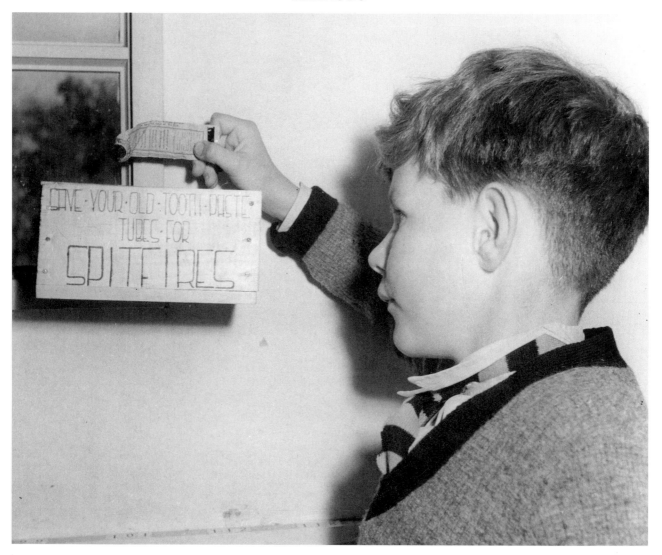

SAVE·YOUR·OLD·TOOTH·PASTE
TUBES·FOR
SPITFIRES

Every little helps There are persistent appeals for salvage, even for empty shaving cream, ointment and toothpaste tubes – which you are requested to take back to your chemist – aluminium saucepans are also in great demand, with 1,000 tons collected in 1940 for the manufacture of fighter planes. Not to mention iron railings. Children are much involved in these crusades

Photo: Robert Hunt

Paper shortage Most things, including paper, are in short supply, so shoppers have to tumble vegetables and fruit willy-nilly into their baskets

Photo: Robert Hunt

Canteen meals A major change in eating habits wrought by the war is the rapid expansion of canteen meals, at work, in the forces, at school. Here, a canteen has been developed beside an Underground shelter for passengers and shelter-seekers alike

Photo: Robert Hunt

Do-it-yourself piggery 'Doing your bit' might embrace part-time civil defence duty and raising vegetables or livestock to supplement the rations . . . a theme well represented by these wartime special policemen busy with their animals

Photo: Robert Hunt

The black market Nylons for sale in Petticoat Lane in London's East End in 1950, probably going for 5s. (25p, or £10 current value). A regime of shortages inevitably spawns a black market during and after the war, mainly small scale, with the 'spiv', such as the one portrayed here, smiled, rather than frowned, upon as an amusing rogue

Photo: Popperphoto

HOME COMFORTS

For many the blacked-out house became a citadel, the criss-crossed taped windows, a sensible precaution against bomb-blasted flying glass, and, for some, the sealed gas-proofed room, adding to the fortress-like image. Long weary hours working and striving to make ends meet left many with little energy to go out in the evening, especially when there was the risk of air raids. The blackout, too, could be perilous – one in five people claimed to have suffered a blackout associated injury in the first four months of the war. It has been said of the blackout that it 'transformed conditions of life more thoroughly than any other single feature of the war'. The BBC had planned for the contingency of war more prudently than most. During the war it became a mighty network, trebling the hours of daily broadcasting to 150 hours and increasing its staff from 4,000 to 115,000. This was, and will remain, the only war in which radio – or, as it then was, wireless – was sovereign. The BBC dispensed calmly authoritative news, courtesy of announcers like Alvar Liddell; official advice and exhortation, like Freddie Grisewood's *Kitchen Front,* and jaunty, morale-boosting light entertainment, with Tommy Handley's *ITMA*, heard by 20 million at home and another 30 millions overseas, still leaving resonances in everyday speech – 'I don't mind if I do'; 'TTFN' – from among its myriad catch-phrases and characters.

Household goods were in short supply. The 'Utility' strategy, whereby designs and prices were narrowly restricted, was vigorously applied to furniture, kitchen utensils, pottery and electrical equipment. A 'dockets' scheme was used to help newly weds, pregnant women and those homeless through bombing acquire 'utility' essentials to set up house. Some designers found in the sparseness of 'utility' directness an aesthetic improvement on the fussy elaboration of the 1930s, but, in any case, the stringent need for 'austerity' in post-war years, and the prior claim of the 'export drive', meant that well into the 1950s household goods were in short supply. Although there was full employment and reasonable wage levels during the war, the purchase of household goods, understandably, fell by two-thirds. The novelist, Susan Cooper, perceptively wrote that, unlike the military side of things with a tidily signed treaty, 'there was no single finishing line for the shortages of food, clothes and fuel'.

Outside the home the tokens of war could not be avoided. War was on the doorstep. Take a peep out and there might be troops or ARP personnel in the street or an anti-aircraft gun or barrage balloon nearby, whilst the walls would be plastered with posters exhorting you to avoid 'careless talk'. – 'Be Like Dad – Keep Mum' ran a well-remembered one – or to contribute to the latest savings campaign, be it for 'Wings for Victory' or 'Salute the Soldier' week. After the war, these were replaced with earnest resolutions, for example, 'Export or Die' and, although lights shone from windows again, households remained somewhat dull and shabby. In the dreadful winter of 1946/47 fuel shortages closed factories and schools and there were days when half of London's commuters could not reach work. The use of electric fires was banned at certain times of the day and parsnips had to be dug from the frozen soil with electric drills. The bombs might have ceased falling, but much discomfort remained.

Anderson shelter survives bombing A vivid example of the soundness of the Anderson shelter's simple design. A bomb has made an almost direct hit, but the occupants of the shelter have survived unscathed

Photo: Robert Hunt

Digging in Hyde Park to fill all those sandbags Hyde Park is a quarry for sand and a site for trenches for shelter. People continue to stroll through, despite the proximity of the war's urgent needs

Photo: Robert Hunt

Signs of warfare come remarkably close to ordinary life Here, just across the way from buildings and sunnily reflected in the water, a barrage balloon gently floats, ready to rise at the call, and thwart possible dive-bomb or low-flying attacks

Photo: Black Star/Robert Hunt

A First World War veteran prepares for Home Guard duty Shades of the musters raised at the time of the Spanish Armada or the Napoleonic threat; up to 2 million Home Guards are recruited to watch for invasion attempts and impede enemy progress. They are originally known as LDV, Local Defence Volunteers, or, in popular parlance, Look, Duck, and Vanish

Photo: Imperial War Museum/Robert Hunt

The Auxiliary Fire Service, Soho Square, London Civil defence workers relax outside this humorously labelled first aid and general ARP post, typical of thousands to be found in every district

Photo: Robert Hunt

Troops everywhere – even in your front garden These are Canadian troops in the middle of a training exercise and parked in the middle of someone's garden

Photo: Black Star/Robert Hunt

Ingenuity wins the day: the coal-gas motor-bike From February 1942, even the basic petrol ration, enough for about 30 miles a week, is withdrawn, so only essential services survive, which, for some, include getting to work. Coal-gas is used as a substitute, particularly by commercial vans, but also more unusually by motor-bikes

Photo: Robert Hunt

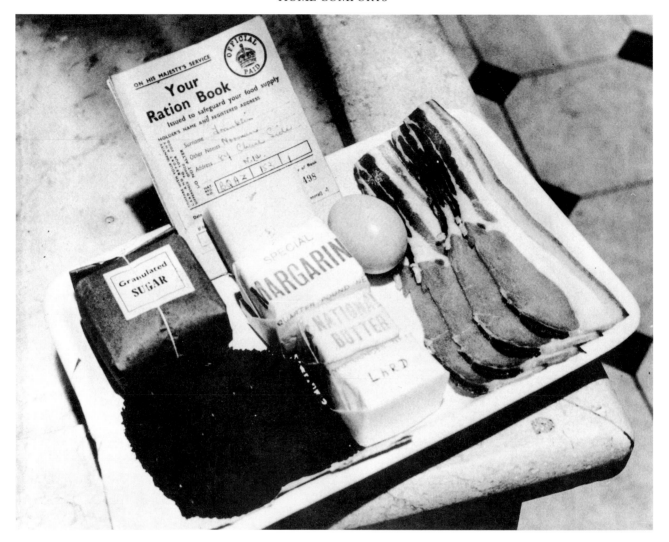

The week's food ration This is actually two weeks' ration and the fortnightly egg was not always forthcoming. However, it supplied a balanced and nourishing diet: the bacon ration was, for instance, more than was on average consumed pre-war

Photo: Mary Evans Picture Library

WOMEN AND CHILDREN

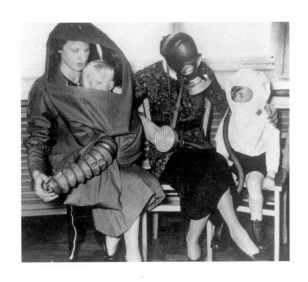

Throughout history war had been grimly seen as man's business. No longer was this the case. In 1939 women and children were pitched right into the front line. Nothing more vividly illustrated this than the sight of gas masks for babies. The youngest British war victim was an eleven-month-baby killed in the Blitz. Women and children were bombed in the towns and machine-gunned in the countryside. Yet the good side was a government's recognition that, in total war, the entire population required urgent help. Rationing was one example – and, on average, we out-caloried the Germans by a daily 3,000 to their 2,000 throughout the war. However, a whole battery of health and welfare benefits was at our disposal, particularly for mothers and children. These included orange juice and cod-liver oil for babies and children, 65,000 day nursery places, 7 million free diphtheria vaccinations, and cheap or free milk as well as improved clinical supervision for schoolchildren. The Emergency Hospital Service, whereby 2,400 of Britain's 3,000 hospitals were nationally co-ordinated, extended free provision, introduced a national blood transfusion scheme and enabled other medical advances: all of which benefited both children and adults. Social policy was grounded in the ethic of state management. The 1942 Beveridge Report, the blueprint for the post-war Welfare State, was broadly welcomed and led to the comprehensive series of national insurance reforms launched in 1948. Although the nation was badly crippled by the war – two-thirds of our export trade had vanished and, in 1946, we spent £300 million more abroad than we earned – the world was lost in admiration, as that same belief in cohesive and collective planning was channelled into organising the National Health Service. Children would gain similarly from the changes in education and the post-war insistence on new school building.

Women adapted quickly to the war effort. Half a million joined the three services, while many more were 'uniformed' in land army breeches or engineering dungarees. One and a half million women – a third of its total workforce – worked in essential industries. Dressing to any level of smartness was a dispiriting task. Clothes rationing was introduced in 1941 on a 'coupons' basis: for example, a woman might need 14 out of a yearly allocation of 48 coupons for an overcoat. 'Make do and mend' was a key propaganda phrase of the era and 'renovation' was the buzz-word of fashionable advice. Many women resorted to making their own clothes, from dress patterns, which remained popular for a long time after the war. Trousers grew more common, the headscarf and turban became universal and styles had a military tone. It would not be until March 1949 that clothes rationing was abolished.

Queuing - a daily occupation Women, along with their small children, queuing for their meat ration at a Southend butchers, although unrationed fish often draws the longest queues

Photo: Black Star/Hunt

Anti-panic war fashion These so-called 'anti-panic' styles, with their martial air of high collars, big buttons, square shoulders, short skirts and practical headgear, are the nearest we come to wartime fashion, at a time when clothing is rationed and undue frippery disliked

Photo: Robert Hunt

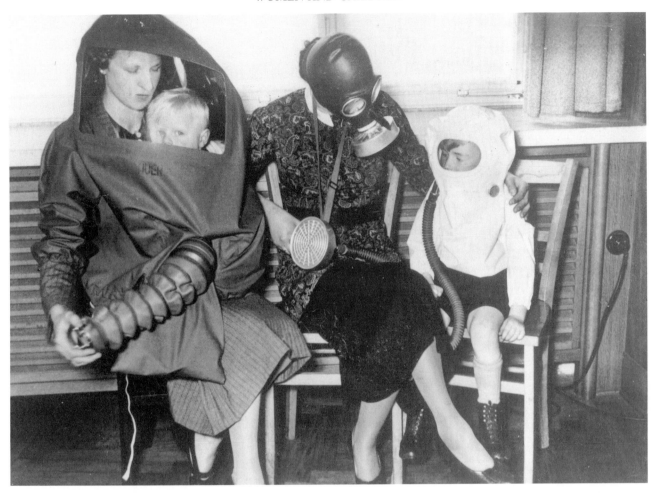

Gas mask parade Among the 38 million gas masks distributed in 1938 are family varieties, including a Mickey Mouse style for young children (not shown here), and the parent-pumped baby contraption for the pram. Rattles, a relic of the First World War, are to sound the sinister warning of gas attacks (which thankfully never happen), although everyone is supposed to carry their gas mask at all time, and children are made to practise wearing them daily at school

Photo: Robert Hunt

WAAF barrack room A normal barrack room, complete with 'beds' [that] will be made up as laid down in standing orders' and a recalcitrant stove: the difference is, of course, that the hut is inhabited by members of the Women's Auxiliary Air Force, many of whom work as radio operators, photographers and bomb plotters, but also as barrage balloon crews and even as ferry pilots delivering planes to airfields

Photo: Kosmos Press Bureau/Robert Hunt

Australian air force girls help out in Britain Although everyone knows how substantial numbers of overseas armed forces arrived in Britain during and after the war, not everybody recalls that these include women. This busy, cheerful group of Australian air force girls are a reminder of this

Photo: Black Star/Robert Hunt

War games War becomes a reality even for small children, who imitate it in their games. After centuries of the French being thought of as Britain's natural foe, the Germans replace them for the duration of the war and several decades afterwards

Photo: Robert Hunt

Queuing for the 'Britain Can Make It' exhibition of 1946 The exhibition at the Victoria and Albert Museum in London had 1.5 million visitors

Photo: Black Star/Robert Hunt

Queuing for the cinema This film is *Target for Tonight*, the 1941 classic semi-documentary, about a Wellington bomber over Germany, which won a special Oscar

Photo: Black Star/Robert Hunt

Queuing for the bus The queue can reach as long as 100 yards, with buses hit by shortages of staff and materials, with bus curfews (none after 9 or 10 p.m.), and with bus tickets reduced in size and thickness

Photo: Black Star/Robert Hunt

Queuing to emigrate Queuing at
the Canadian Embassy in the
immediate post-war years

Photo: Black Star/Robert Hunt

ON PLEASURE BENT

Expenditure on recreation doubled during the war, a tendency that continued afterwards. For all that people were engaged in long hours of arduous toil and duty, and for all that many, fatigued and fearful of bombs and blackout, stayed close to home, there was an alternative reaction. When war came knocking at the front door, it caused many to think only of the day and to seek release. Then, with the war over, there was a natural sense of relief, as witnessed in the nationwide victory celebrations. And with rationing and shortages continuing, alongside full employment and steady wages, there was little on which to spend one's money apart from leisure.

Popular music was essentially dance band music. It was heard on the radio in daily programmes like *Music While You Work* and sung along with in factories. It was danced to by thousands, not only in the urban *palais de danse*, but in hundreds of church halls and on as many camp sites. The song most requested of cinema organists was *White Cliffs of Dover* and that brand of decent sentiment was very much in vogue. The light theatre remained attractive, although much of its attention was turned, mainly through the ENSA organisation, to providing the troops and munitions workers with colourful shows, albeit of varying quality. ENSA provided 2.5 million shows during the war, watched by over 300 million war workers and service personnel. An interesting sidelight on leisure exhibited a further twist in the psychology of war. Many people sought rather serious diversion. The BBC's *Brains Trust* drew an unlikely audience of 12 million listeners, while, a tiny but illuminating fact, the army's Southern Command had thirty chamber music groups in rehearsal just prior to D-Day.

The cinema was a major source of pleasure. Every week in Britain 30 million cinema tickets were sold. Seventy-five per cent of adults, and an even greater proportion of children were cinema-goers. Many went once a week, sometimes ritually, to the same cinema on the same night; two out of five teenagers went twice or more. By 1946, a third of the population went to the 'flicks' once a week and possibly a sixth twice or more. After the early shocks of war, crowds swarmed to sporting events. Full houses of 133,000 gathered at Hampden Park for the England *v.* Scotland Victory football internationals and 414,000 attended the 1945 programme of thirty days' major cricket at Lord's, whereas only 330,000 had watched the full offering of first-class cricket in 1939. The Lord's ground record is 90,000: it was for the 1945 Victory Test. The boom continued after the war. In the glorious 1947 summer, made famous by the 'Middlesex Twins', Denis Compton and Bill Edrich, 3 million watched first-class cricket, an amazing average approaching 10,000 a day for each match played.

With the pressures of war over, along with its dearth of transport and never quite convincing concept of 'holidays at home', visitors flocked to the familiar resorts, whilst Butlin's Holiday Camps, with their intriguingly shrewd 'regimental' *bonhomie*, had a striking appeal. In 1951 the British took 27 million holidays. With clothes rationing on its way out, women were able at last to indulge in the longer, more feminine New Look, which coincided with their return to more 'feminine' domesticated roles.

ENSA concert on an airfield Entertainment is ubiquitous. Here a small ENSA concert party turns a piece of board into a stage and brings a few moments' gaiety to this aerodrome: they are a small part of the 80% of show business people who have some involvement with ENSA, and this is just one of 2.5 million shows arranged by ENSA during the war

Photo: Robert Hunt

An al fresco dance in the countryside Soldiers play the instruments for their comrades dancing with domestic servants from a stately home, which, like dozens of others, has been commandeered for war purposes

Photo: Robert Hunt

Wartime dance hall Ballroom dancing, which grew in popularity after the First World War, is a major source of respite and fun during the Second, with local town halls, school halls, church halls and military premises transformed into *palais de danse*, often, as in this case, with the dance band in uniform

Photo: Robert Hunt

Myra Hess playing at the National Gallery Dame Myra Hess plays the piano at one of her legendary one shilling (5p.) lunchtime concerts, frequently of German music, in a crowded, if bomb-damaged National Gallery, from which all the paintings have been removed to a place of safety

Photo: G.H. Metcalf Black Star/Robert Hunt

Arsenal v. Charlton at White Hart Lane, November 1940 With almost empty stands, football continues to be played during one of the worst phases of the war

Photo: Popperphoto

Queuing again, this time for the theatre This queue queues patiently for two hours to see Leo Marks' play, *The Girl who Couldn't Quite*, at the King's Theatre, Hammersmith, shortly after the war

Photo: Black Star/Robert Hunt

VE Day celebrations On 8 May 1945, cheering crowds in Whitehall hail the victor, Winston Churchill on Victory for Europe day

Photo: Popperphoto

Holiday crowds at Blackpool After the war many people seek the kind of seaside holiday they favoured in the 1930s: it will be some years before the rush to Spanish beaches begins

Photo: Popperphoto

The 1948 Olympic Games are hosted in London The Games are a Herculean effort in difficult conditions to reassure everyone that the war is really over. Here Fanny Blankers Koen, the Flying Dutchwoman, is the much-lauded star, winning, a record at this time, four gold medals

Photo: Popperphoto

After wartime austerity: The New Look The more fitted styling and longer skirt, created by Dior in 1947, is a feminine reaction to the sartorial drudgery of the 1940s. A shop assistant measures the fabled 14 inches in a Richards dress shop in London, 1948

Photo: Popperphoto

LIBERTY HALL

The war supplied the key to Liberty Hall. In the immediate prewar years, an average of three out of ten mothers conceived their first child out of wedlock, although 70% of these were legitimised by marriage. During the war the chance to marry – and the willingness – was reduced and that figure dropped to under 40%. Illegitimate births tripled to an annual 16 per thousand single women. The famous 'baby boom' began with an average of 16 or 17 births per thousand head of population in 1942, and peaked in 1947 at over 20. Equally shocklng for old-time morality was the growth of divorce. The figure for the 1940s and early 1950s is three times that of the 1930s, with an astounding leap to 60,000 in 1947.

For millions, horizons suddenly changed: both men and women were left lonely, or caught up in new relationships, so creating this more tempestuous dynamic of social life. Some 100,000 women married servicemen from allied or Dominion countries, as well as 80,000 who became 'GI brides'. The fact that more women worked, many in jobs previously regarded as a male province, was a great emancipator. Habits altered. Pub-going is one example where, midway through the war, many women joined their male companions in their locals – an activity formerly frowned upon, as film-going or sport on a Sunday was, or women wearing trousers. As the war advanced, and the American dancing styles – jitterbugging, for instance – were introduced, these, too, were regarded as 'sinful' by the older generations.

Another sign of this increased openness was a rise in more candid displays of affection and passion. With three out of five women having near-relatives in the armed forces, some half a million of whom were killed or maimed, there was a sense of uncertainty, of wanting to find some completeness or purpose to life before it was too late. It understandably led to what Barbara Cartland called 'the quick, rush wedding of wartime'. Over 22 in a thousand of the population were married in 1939/1940 and, after a decline, this number rose again to 19 by the late 1940s, with three out of ten marriages involving young women under 21. This relaxation of the national stern moral fibre was reflected in its entertainments. There was much lighter fare even from the once forbidding BBC. Attitudes remained slightly prurient. The fabled continuity – 'we never closed' – of London's Windmill Theatre underpins the point. During and after the war, its stationary nudes were somehow a symbol of a semi-permissive mentality: yes, you could look at naked showgirls, but, no, they mustn't move. The newspapers began to be more adventurous. One 'naughty' war-time legend was Jane. Born Chrystabel Leighton-Porter, she was made famous as the model for the Pett strip cartoon in *the Daily Mirror*, complete with Fritz the dachshund. Her antics in varied stages of undress made her an enormously favourite 'pin-up' (another typically 1940s' word) with the forces.

The strait-laced codes of prewar Britain diminished. The door of Liberty Hall would not easily be shut again.

Busy at her lathe: the woman engineer Before the war this would have been a contradiction in terms . . . so eagerly have women taken up such tasks that, by the middle of the war, 1.5 million women are members of trades unions, including nearly 150,000 in the hitherto anti-female Amalgamated Engineering Union. This one is helping to make Spitfires

Photo: Robert Hunt

A public embrace It is 1945 and a sailor, about to set sail, bids his sweetheart a passionate and public farewell, with the official on the left unsure whether to disapprove or be envious. The emotional turmoil and snatched courtships of the war sees some of the old taboos, such as public displays of conspicuous affection, vanish

Photo: The Hulton Getty Picture Collection Ltd

GI Brides sail to America The GI brides sailing away to join their husbands in America will often be disappointed to discover on arrival that America is not the version they have seen in Hollywood films

Photo: Popperphoto

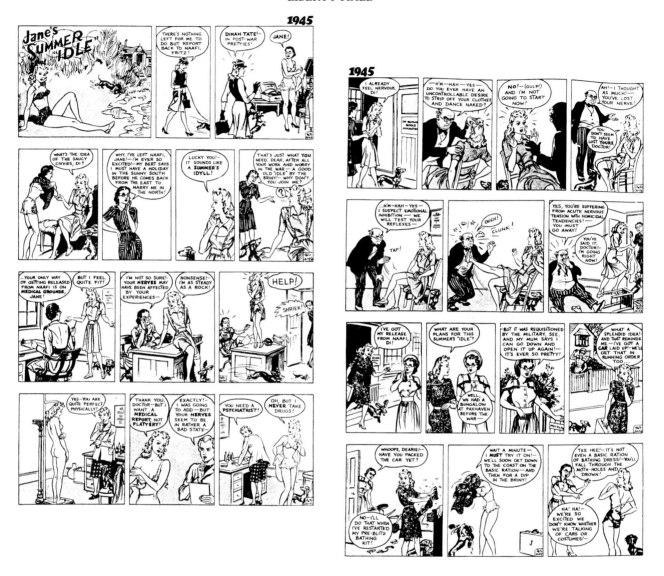

Britain's secret weapon: Jane Jane, typically finding ways of saucily revealing her curves in 1945 mode. Such is the popularity of Norman Pett's light-hearted cartoon in the *Daily Mirror* that Winston Churchill describes her as 'Britain's secret weapon'. And then she is thought by many to be partly responsible for his defeat in the 1945 General Election, because she has insured that the Labour-supporting *Mirror* will be read by thousands in the armed forces

Photo: Daily Mirror

The Forties' macabre side The Christie Murders, with their dingy background and undertones of strange sexuality come to light at his trial in 1953 and make the address of 10 Rillington Place the most infamous in Britain . . . even banishing the death of Queen Mary to the middle pages

Photo: Daily Mirror

Jitterbugging Feldman's Swing Club in London in 1947. This couple, to quote the original caption, 'delight the swing crazy crowd with a routine jitterbug'. The sedate formalism of ballroom dancing is irrevocably challenged by such American influences

Photo: Popperphoto

THE REAL END OF THE WAR

So, given the social continuum from the war to the post-war years, when was the real watershed? The signs of what late twentieth-century life would be like first became apparent in the early 1950s. The passing of the great reforming Attlee administration in 1951 ended over a decade of collective endeavour and, with improving conditions, there was a gradual end to rationing and other controls. Internationally, the end of Empire, and events like the traumatic Suez Crisis of 1956, marked Britain's decline as a global power more than the peace of 1945. Nonetheless, the 1951 Festival of Britain gave the nation a shot in the arm. With its mix of South Bank exhibition and Battersea fun-fair, each attracting over 8 million visitors, it was immensely popular. Michael Frayn concluded that it was 'a rainbow – a brilliant sign riding the storm and promising fairer weather'. The fairer weather included many more cars – the 2 million vehicles on the roads in both 1939 and 1948 suddenly rose to 6 million by 1960 - and more consumer durables – less than one in ten households had a washing-machine in the early 1950s; it was almost seven in ten households by the late 1960s. Many more holidays were taken and there were the beginnings of regular foreign holidays – by the 1960s one in six holidays would be taken abroad. Equally, newcomers arrived on our shores. During the 1950s some 150,000 Jamaicans came to Britain, presaging the multicultural society of today.

Social attitudes changed and social disciplines eased. The teddy boys of the mid 1950s gave the first clue to youth's detachment from society at large. 'Purple heart' pills appeared in 1951, a mild portent of modern drug usage, while in 1954 the idea of the contraceptive pill – that most dramatic sexual liberator – hit the headlines. It was in the mid 1950s that the abrasive notes of Rock'n'roll were heard and pop culture was introduced to the United Kingdom. There was a whole series of cultural touchstones, such as Kingsley Amis's *Lucky Jim* (1954) and John Osborne's *Look Back in Anger* (1956), that rejected old values and embraced new ones.

If one were to seize on just one occasion to distinguish the switch from war and its aftermath to a brave new world, it must be the Coronation of Queen Elizabeth II in 1953. It marked the beginning of the New Elizabethan Age. By happy conjunction, a set of characteristically British triumphs ushered in the era. There was Stanley Matthews winning his sole FA Cup medal, Gordon Richards winning his only Derby, the England cricket team regaining the Ashes from their Australian rivals, and Sherpa Tensing and Edmund Hillary's conquest of Mount Everest. There was a deeper reason still. The Coronation was the breakthrough point for television in this country. It was the genuine start of a national culture based on television.

A.J.P. Taylor, not an historian given to sentimental judgements, said that, during the Second World War, 'the British people came of age' and remained 'tolerant, patient and generous'. It is a verdict that might well stand muster for the first years of peacetime, when the majority, while stoically grumbling, accepted the arduous task of peace making as readily as they had that of war making. Now Britain turned from its 'finest hours' to the new challenges of the second half of the century.

Festival of Britain, 1951 A sunny day on the South Bank, with visitors around the Dome of Discovery, and with 'the luminous exclamation mark' of the Skylon to the right. The Festival shows justifiable pride in past achievments and looks ahead to the transformations that are to come in the Sixties

Photo: Topham Picturepoint

Gridlock on the Kingston bypass Whitsun weekend, May 1950: an early sign of that automotive nightmare, the gridlocked road, that will characterise the rest of the century and beyond

Photo: Popperphoto

The Ashes for England England skipper Len Hutton, the then customary cigarette in hand, acknowledges the adulation of a huge Oval crowd, celebrating England's defeat of Australia and the return of the long-absent Ashes to this country in 1953. It is one of several significant achievements in Coronation year

Photo: Popperphoto

Coal mines nationalised in 1947
Two women are appointed to
the National Coal Board to
represent domestic consumers.
Here one of them, a former
mayoress of Hackney, receives
her first official communication
from a female dispatch rider
(another breakthrough)

Photo: Black Star/Robert Hunt

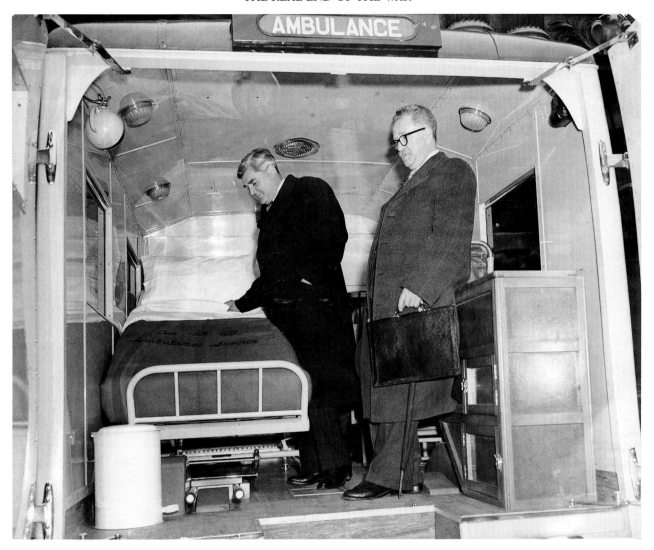

The foundation of the National Health Service Aneurin Bevan, in July 1948, inspecting a brand new ambulance, symbol of the progressive approach to the people's health. Within a year of its inception, 95% of the population are covered by the NHS; 8.5 million have had much-needed dental treatment, and over 5 million pairs of spectacles have been dispensed to people who had hitherto been unable to afford them

Photo: Topham Picturepoint

Teddy boys in the Old Kent Road, London Teddy boys are hanging about between the old style restaurant and the cinema posters. Thus begins the post-war phenomenon of the youth cult, with mods and rockers, skinheads and so on to follow

Photo: Popperphoto

Gordon Richards wins the Derby On 6 June 1953, exactly eight years after D-Day, the young new queen (in her New Look coat) congratulates the veteran jockey who, mounted on 'Pinza' has just won his first and only Epsom Derby

Photo: Popperphoto

The Coronation, 2 June 1953 We listened to George VI's coronation on the wireless, the first and last such event where the radio was king; we watch his daughter's coronation on television

Photo: Robert Hunt

A group of Servicemen and women in Berlin This occasion marks the real turning-point to a future filled with hope

Photo: Popperphoto